BIRD·CARVING Basics

Volume Five

TEXTURING

BIRD·CARVING Basics
Volume Five

TEXTURING

Curtis J. Badger

STACKPOLE BOOKS

Published by
STACKPOLE BOOKS
Cameron and Kelker Streets
P.O. Box 1831
Harrisburg, PA 17105

Printed in the United States of America

10 9 8 7 6 5 4 3 2 1

First edition

*Cover design by Tracy Patterson with
Caroline Miller*

Interior design by Marcia Lee Dobbs

Cover photo: Rich Smoker burning a mallard wing.
Photographed by Curtis Badger.

Library of Congress Cataloging-in-Publication Data

Badger, Curtis J.
    Bird carving basics.

    Contents: Vol. 1. Eyes — [etc.] — v. 5. Texturing
    — v. 6. Painting.
    1. Wood-carving. 2. Birds in art. I. Title.
TT199.7.B33   1990   731.4'62   90–9491
ISBN 0–8117–2334–8 (v. 1)

Contents

Acknowledgments   vii

Introduction   ix

1   **Texturing a Decorative Bufflehead Pair**
    Don Mason   1

2   **Feather Detail for a California Quail**
    Dan Brown   31

3   **Texturing a Crow with Rasp and Gouge**
    Grayson Chesser   45

4   **Comb-Painting a Pintail**
    Grayson Chesser   63

5   **Burning and Stoning a Decorative Scaup**
    Rich Smoker   73

Acknowledgments

A series such as this would not be possible without the generous cooperation of artists such as Don Mason, Dan Brown, Grayson Chesser, and Rich Smoker. Not only did they let me peer over their shoulders with my camera as they worked, but later they took the time to review the resulting photographs and explain each intricate step in the carving process. Thanks for your patience, guys.

In writing this series, I've yet to meet a carver who was reluctant to share his or her carving techniques. The reason, perhaps, is that wildfowl art is a sharing process. Art doesn't exist in a vacuum; even the most talented artists have learned from others, and all the carvers I've met have been more than willing to pass along their expertise to beginners.

Bird carving has grown in popularity in recent years because most carvers are willing and able teachers. All four artists included in this book have conducted workshops, taught in college classes, or provided private instruction to beginning carvers. Wildfowl art seems to epitomize the old practice of apprenticeship; the more advanced artisan is always willing to share techniques with the beginner.

The four carvers included in this volume are also outstanding artists, each with his individual interpretation of wildfowl art. I appreciate their assistance in making this book possible, and in spreading enthusiasm for birds and bird art.

Introduction

This is a book about the craft of bird carving. It is a book about technique, and it presents a varied menu of methods for achieving the same end: creating the illusion of feathers and feather patterns.

What we have here is a series of options, ranging from traditional methods used by decoy makers a century ago to the tools and techniques available today.

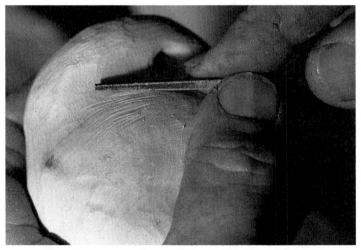

Here, carver Dan Brown illustrates a technique used in the 1950s by the noted carvers Steve and Lem Ward of Crisfield, Maryland. A small triangular file is used to lightly scribe feather lines along the head of a bird. "Sometimes Lem would actually heat the file and bend it so he could reach tight areas better," says Dan.

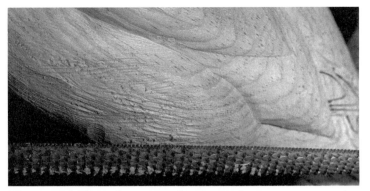

Many old-time decoy makers used a coarse rasp to reduce the reflectivity of the paint.

Modern carvers can use a rotary rasp on a Foredom tool to create a textured surface on their hunting decoys.

One method is not more correct or proper than the other, except in how it pertains to you and what you're trying to accomplish through bird carving. It could be that Grayson Chesser's traditional method of using rasps and gouges lends itself to what you're trying to express. Or the contemporary technique of stoning and burning might be more in keeping with your visual goals. We're presenting the menu, and it's strictly up to you to select the entree that best matches your appetite.

The ability to add feather texture to carved birds has transformed wildfowl art in the past twenty years. Not long ago, most carved birds were "slicks," untextured hunting decoys painted to provide the illusion of feathers and feather groups. Today, with high-speed grinders and an almost unlimited variety of stones

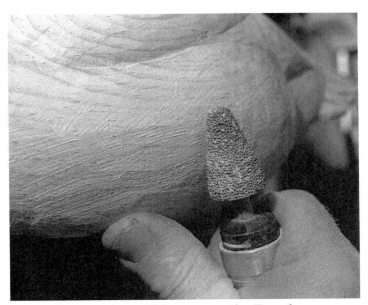

A cylindrical Kutz-all cutter on the Foredom produces an effect similar to the rasp. "When making hunting decoys, you can texture the surface with one of these cutters and paint the bird without sanding," says Dan.

This teal hen, showing realistic texturing along the head and breast, was carved by Dan Brown, who used texturing stones in a variety of shapes to replicate the feathers.

and cutters, carvers can make a piece of wood appear soft and billowy. And fine-tipped burning pens can accurately duplicate every feather, right down to the last quill and barb. These two tools, when used in combination, can render feather texture that is remarkably lifelike.

Of course, a bird is more than a collection of feathers. For a carving to be truly lifelike, it must capture something essential about a bird that goes beyond the replication of feathers. The best of the old-time decoy makers were able to capture the essence of a species of waterfowl because they observed birds on an almost daily basis and studied them closely. Such study and attention to behavioral nuances is still necessary today, despite our wonderful collection of tools.

Tools have transformed wildfowl art, making possible all sorts of visual exploration. Not long ago, carvers who wanted to replicate feathers had to resort to comparatively crude methods. Many carvers used rasps to create featherlike flow lines. Some used tiny files and gouges to create detail.

Although feather texture today is considered part of the realm of decorative carving, texturing was also important in making hunting decoys a century ago. A fairly accurate representation of feathers made a bird more lifelike, but texture also helped in other practical matters. In the early morning sunlight, a decoy bobbing about on the water could shine like a warning buoy. A textured surface made the decoy less likely to reflect light. Some of the old factory decoys, like the Victor Animal Trap decoys, were painted with the lathe marks left intact. No, these marks don't look that much like feathers, but the texture is an advantage. Besides, eliminating sanding cut a costly step in production.

Learning carving techniques is not automatically going to make you a wildfowl artist. This series presents a variety of choices as to craft, and how you apply that craft is up to you. Choosing a method of carving is only a first step; you must eventually add your own feelings and experiences to technical virtuosity to create a carving that is uniquely your own.

This miniature mallard drake is a factory decoy made by the Victor Animal Trap company. Rather than sanding the decoys smooth, the marks were left on to suggest texturing and reduce the possibility of glare.

The sessions in this book represent methods that have worked for others. Finding methods that work for you is part of the exciting exploration of learning, and we hope this series will help, or at least provide a few shortcuts.

Learning carving technique is much like learning a language. First you master the vocabulary, the tenses, the sentence structure, and then you begin to communicate. Art is a process of having something to say, and then determining how best to express yourself. This book provides the rudiments of communication, but what you choose to say is up to you.

1

Don Mason
Texturing a Decorative Bufflehead Pair

Until 1982, Don Mason spent most of his spare time driving dirt track stock cars. When he wasn't driving he was tinkering, attempting to squeeze a few extra horsepower from a souped-up Chevy.

In 1982 Don quit the racing circuit—too expensive, he says—and began looking for another avocation. He happened by the Ward Foundation Wildfowl Art Exhibition in Salisbury, Maryland, that October while on his way to a race in Dover, Delaware, and he immediately became hooked on bird carving. It's an unusual transition, going from stock car racing to bird carving, but that's the way it happened for Don. "I bought a copy of Bruce Burk's book (*Game Bird Carving*) that day at the Ward Show, and I went home and carved a bufflehead," he says.

Since then, Don has converted his basement into a carving studio, and the only remnants of his racing career are a few snapshots tacked to his studio wall. His home, which overlooks the seaside marshes of Virginia's Eastern Shore, is filled with his carvings and ribbons won at a variety of carving competitions.

Don, who works in electronics at NASA, took a workshop with Pat Godin in Salisbury in 1985, and has worked diligently at developing his technique. For the past two years he has competed in the open (professional) class and has chalked up wins at the Ward World Championship in Ocean City, Maryland, at the Mid-Atlantic in Virginia Beach, and at shows in Richmond, Chestertown, and Tuckerton, New Jersey.

Don specializes in realistic birds and uses a wide variety of reference material, including cast study parts, photographs, and videotapes. In this session, he is texturing a pair of bufflehead ducks. The birds have been carved, the eyes have been inserted, and feather flow lines and feather patterns have been sketched in order for Don to previsualize how the finished birds will look. He works from fairly detailed patterns, sketching not only the outline of the birds, but adding feather detail as well. The sketching process helps him determine what will or will not work in wood. He uses mounted birds and photographs as references in determining feather placement and patterns.

Don will texture the bufflehead in two steps. First, he will begin by using stoning tools to relieve each feather, separate the primaries, and provide a foundation for the intricate feather burning that will come later. The stoning process is shown on the bufflehead hen.

The burning process will be demonstrated on the bufflehead drake, which is depicted in a sleeping pose. Taking advantage of his background in electronics, Don makes his own burning tools, using fine, 20-gauge nickel-chromium wire for a tip. These fine tips can yield up to 120 burn lines per inch, enabling him to add an extraordinary amount of detail to each feather. Both birds are carved from tupelo.

Establishing the flow lines is an important first step in the texturing process because these lines determine the placement and pattern of feathers, and will later affect the painting process. This photo shows how the lines sweep across the sidepockets. A mounted bird was used as reference in sketching these lines.

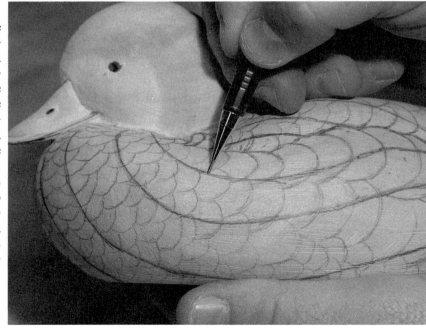

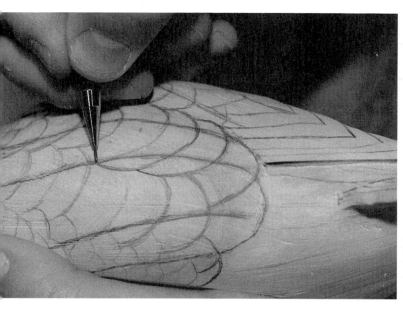

After Don determines the flow lines, he draws individual feathers, which will later be relieved with various stoning tools.

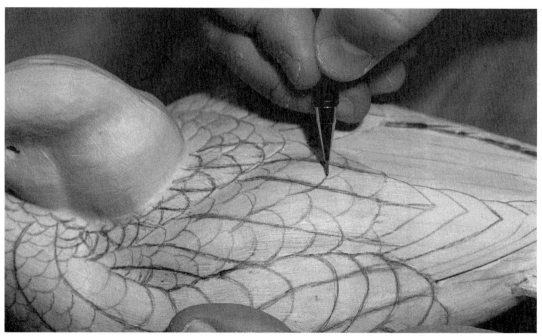

This photo shows the feather layout along the wings of the bufflehead, as well as in the cape area behind the head.

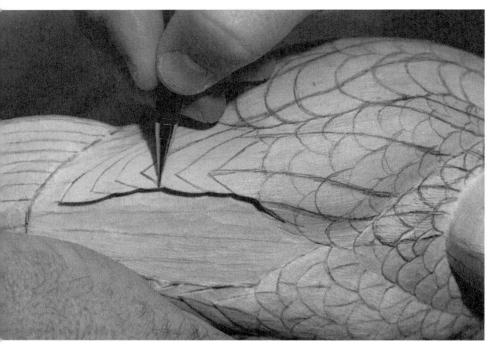

Don sketches
the inner
portion of the
primary
feathers, then
undercuts
the line with
a burning
tool to provide
definition.

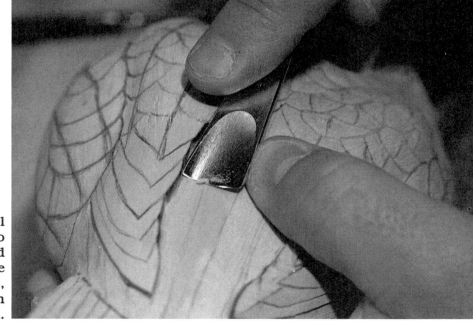

A broad chisel
is used to
remove wood
between the
primaries,
making them
appear raised.

Now that the flow lines and feather patterns have been sketched, the bufflehead hen is ready for stoning. Don works from a fairly detailed sketch, which also serves as a pattern when roughing out the birds.

He uses several different stoning tips on his high-speed grinder. These are three of his favorites. The cutter on the left is a standard ruby cutter; at center is a rasplike "stump cutter" popularized by the late world champion carver John Scheeler; and on the right is a diamond cutter.

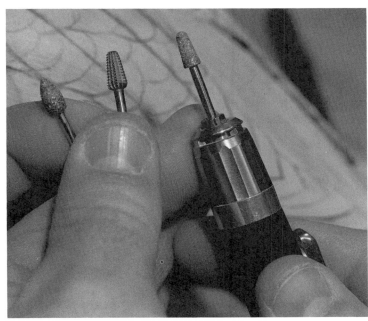

Don begins with a slightly rounded diamond cutter to undercut each feather on the sidepockets, using the sketched lines as a guide. He begins at the back of the bird and works forward.

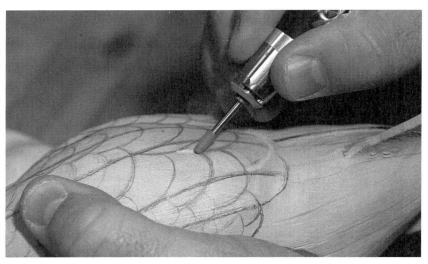

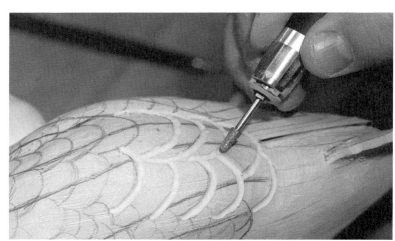

The sidepockets of the bufflehead have two groups of feathers: an upper group of large feathers, and a lower group of smaller feathers. At this stage, Don has undercut the feathers in the upper group, following the sketch lines.

Don now changes to a ruby cutter, which is slightly coarser and more pointed than the diamond tip. Here he undercuts the front portion of each feather, creating a "stairstep" layering of feathers along the sidepocket.

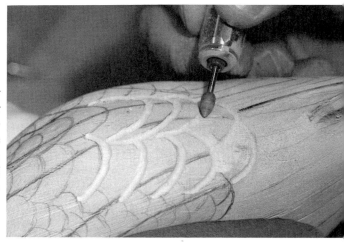

After undercutting the fronts of the feathers, Don goes back to the pencil, resketching the outer lines. "You'll sketch in detail, then grind it all off, and then sketch it in again to go to the next step," says Don.

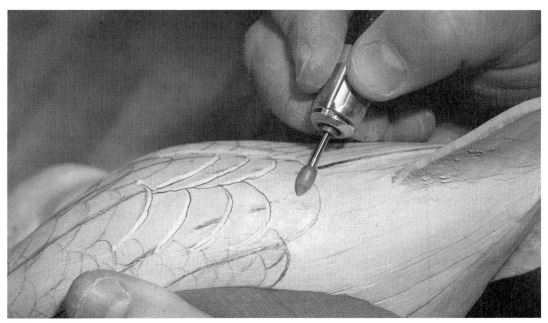

Undercutting the fronts of the feathers has given a layered effect to the sidepocket feathers. Now he uses the ruby cutter to round off and soften the rear edges of each feather.

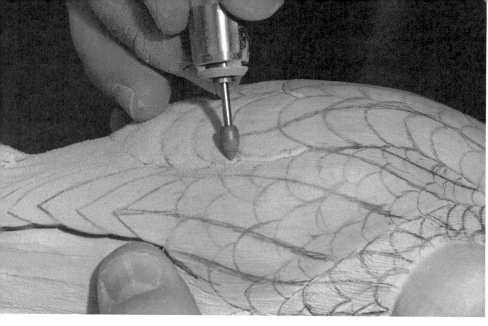

"You want to end up with 'humped' areas, not a scaly effect," Don explains. By rounding off the edges of the feathers with the ruby cutter, the feathers are defined, but are not too obvious.

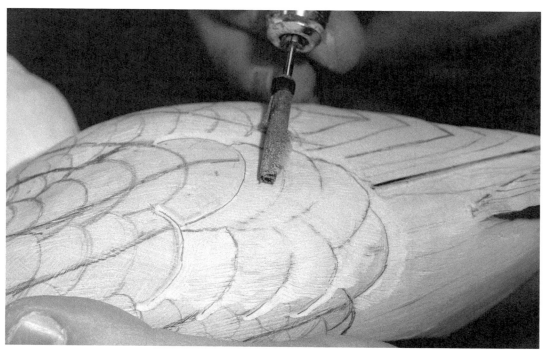

After using the ruby cutter to define the feathers, he places a mandrel with sandpaper in the grinder and lightly sands away the grinding marks left by the ruby cutter.

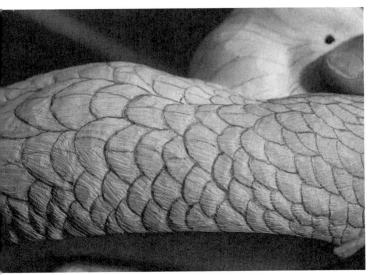

The finished sidepockets and breast area look like this. Don has shaped each feather with the grinding tool, and he has redefined them with the pencil. The next step will be to texture them.

Before texturing the side-pocket feathers, Don will carve the primary feathers. He uses this flat-tipped diamond cutter on his high-speed grinder.

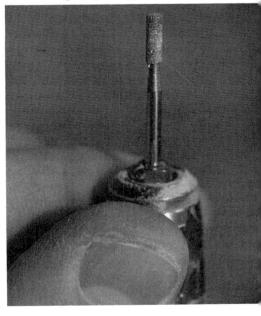

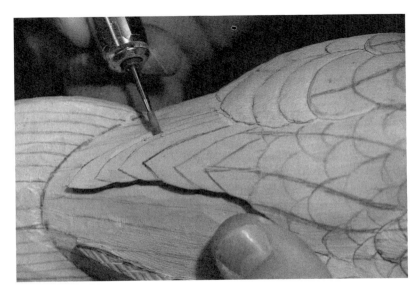

He begins with the lower feathers, following the sketch lines, undercutting each feather.

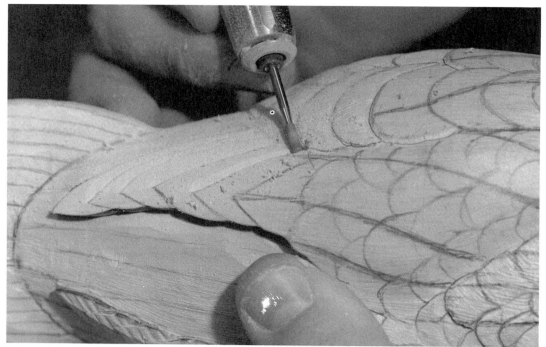

As Don works up the primary stack, undercutting the outer edge of each feather, the feathers take on a layered look.

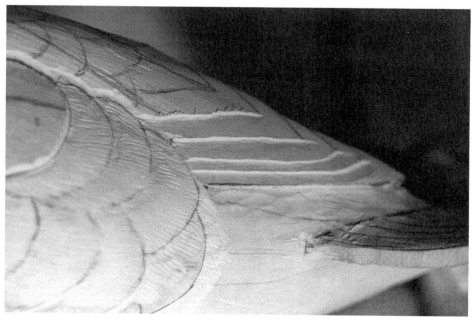

This side view shows the layering effect yielded by undercutting the outer edges of the feathers.

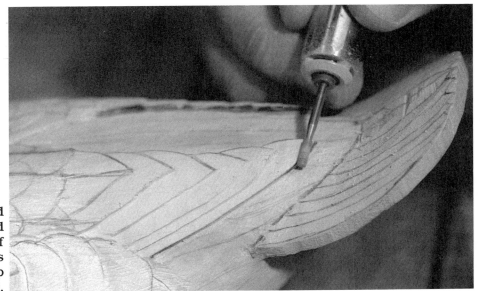

The diamond tip is used to round off the feathers along the group of primaries.

The completed primaries are ready for detailing.

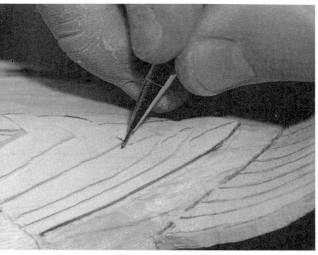

He changes to a slightly more pointed diamond cutter to add some ripples to the inner portions of the primaries. The outer parts of the primaries will be stiff, but the insides of the feathers will have some subtle bumps.

Don uses a pencil to sketch the position of the quills of the primary feathers.

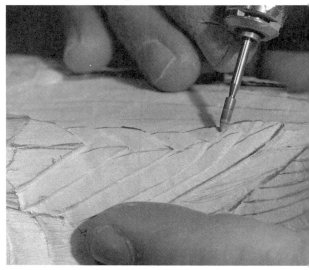

The effect of ripples along the inner primaries is subtle but important. It will show up better after the burning stage.

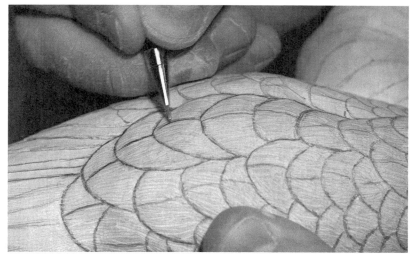

Don now goes back to the side-pockets, using the pencil to draw quills on each of the feathers where quills will show. For reference he uses a mounted bird or a sharp photograph.

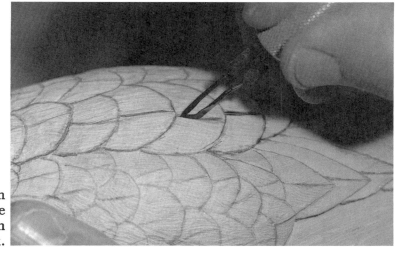

The burning tool is used on fairly low heat to define the quill. Don cuts a line on each side of the pencil mark.

The quills have been cut on each sidepocket feather.

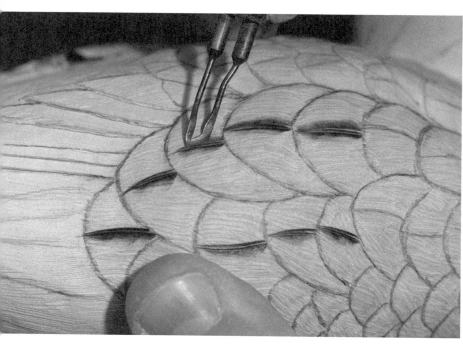

With the quills cut, Don adds a little more heat to the burning tool and uses it to further define each quill by pushing wood away from both sides of the quill. The tip of the tool is inserted in the line and rolled outward.

The completed quills appear to be slightly raised.

Don uses the pencil to draw flow lines on the feathers, deciding at this point where to make feather splits and overlaps. He doesn't sketch the flow lines for all feathers, just enough to get a general idea of the feather layout.

He now inserts in his grinder a stone with a slightly rounded tip that will be used for making feather splits and ripples.

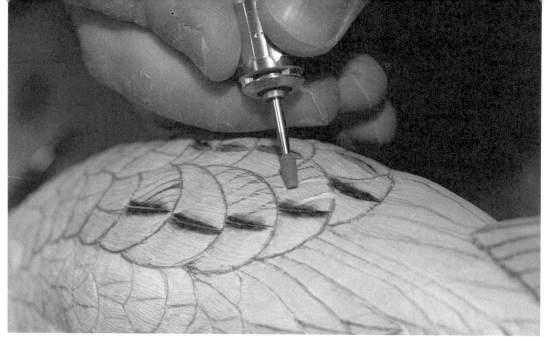

He begins by using the grinder to create feather splits and overlaps. Duck feathers are not perfect, and splits and slightly ragged edges provide a touch of realism.

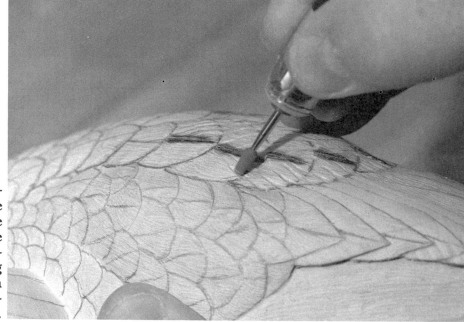

The splits, overlaps, and little ripples should be added before the feathers are detailed. Sketching them first in pencil helps determine location.

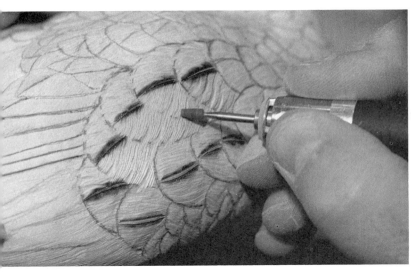

Don has changed back to the sharp, tapered diamond stone to grind barbs onto the feathers of the sidepockets. This photo shows the quills and barbs at the grinding stage. Burning will add even more detail.

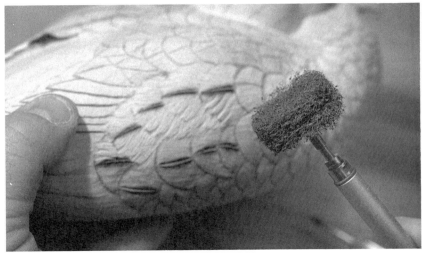

He uses a "de-fuzzing" pad on his grinder to clean the detail produced by the stones. The pad is similar in texture to a household pot scrubber.

The stoned detail after being de-fuzzed. The pad removes dust and wood particles and polishes the area. Don will repeat the stoning and polishing procedure until all the feathers in the sidepocket area have been defined.

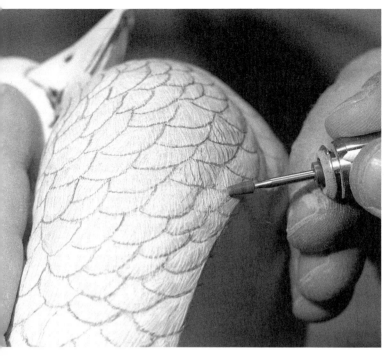

He now begins detailing the breast, using the sharp diamond stone. Unlike the sidepocket area, the breast consists mainly of small feathers, only the ends of which show. There will be no quills in this area, only a series of slightly curved lines to provide the illusion of fine feather barbs.

Don continues this stoning technique throughout the breast area until all feathers are defined. The stoned area looks like this after having been smoothed and cleaned with the de-fuzzing tool.

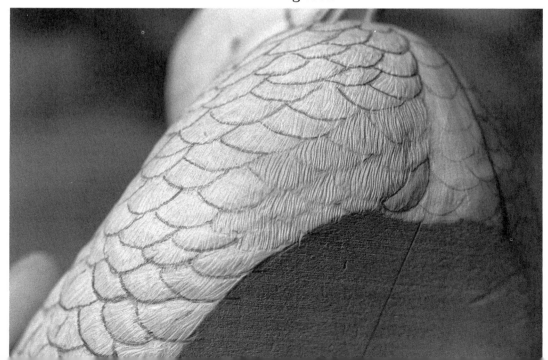

Don is ready to begin burning. He will demonstrate his burning technique on the companion bird to the one used in the stoning sequence, a sleeping bufflehead drake. The drake, with its bill tucked under a wing, has been completely stoned. Note the position of the quills along the sides and just in front of the tail feathers.

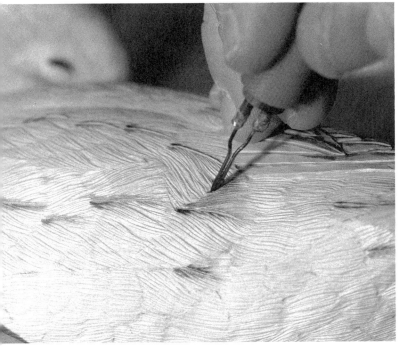

Don begins burning on the sidepockets with a fine tip set at medium low heat. This tip was made from very fine, 20-gauge nickel-chromium wire similar to that used in heater coils. Similar tools are available commercially from carving supply companies.

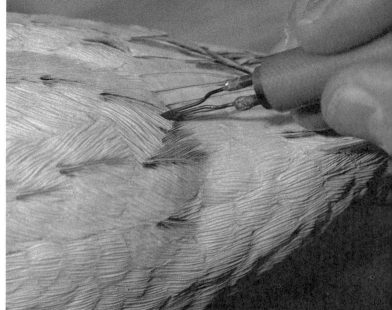

He starts burning at the back of the sidepocket and works forward. "Progress from the lower feathers to the top feathers to get a layered appearance," advises Don. "Usually this means working from the back of the bird to the front of the bird."

The motion of the burning tip should be a "sweeping S," Don says. The feather barb, as it comes off the quill, will be in the shape of a "lazy S." Where splits occur in feathers, he burns detail in the bottom feather, which shows through the split in the top feather.

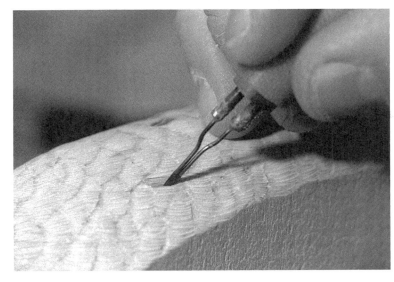

The burning on the breast area consists of a series of fairly short, slightly curved lines to fill each feather. A fine tip on the burning tool is needed for this procedure.

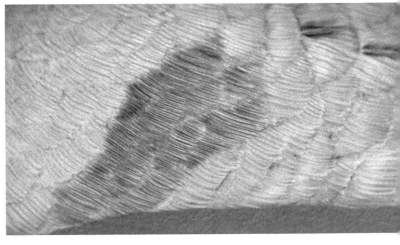

A section of the breast area has been burned with the very fine tip. With the finest tip, Don can get up to 120 burn lines per inch. Average is 80 to 90 lines. "The only disadvantage to burning so finely is that paint tends to fill in the detail," he says. "You have to work with very thin washes of paint."

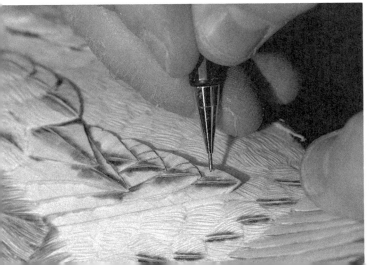

After finishing the breast, he begins burning the primaries. "I usually don't do much stoning on the primaries and tertials. They tend to be very rigid feathers, and you want them to have a fairly smooth surface."

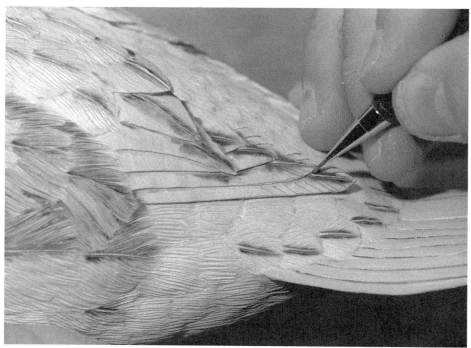

Don draws the barbs on the primaries. "The top side of the primaries will have barbs in a lazy S curve, but the shorter barbs on the bottom will have just a very gentle bend, not an S curve," he points out.

Don now begins working with the burning tool. "You want just enough heat to slightly char the wood," he says. "You don't want a deep burn."

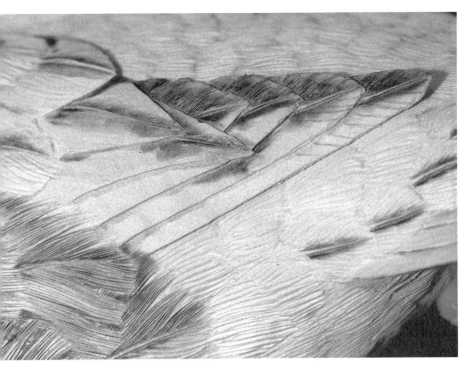

The burning is complete on the upper portion of the primaries, and now Don will burn the lower halves of the feathers.

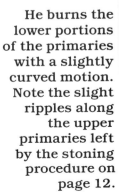

He burns the lower portions of the primaries with a slightly curved motion. Note the slight ripples along the upper primaries left by the stoning procedure on page 12.

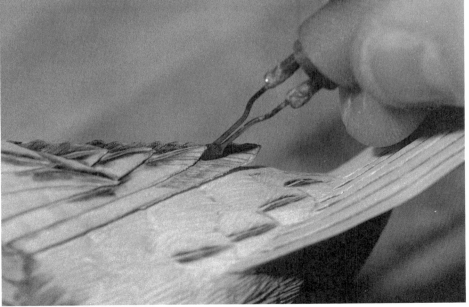

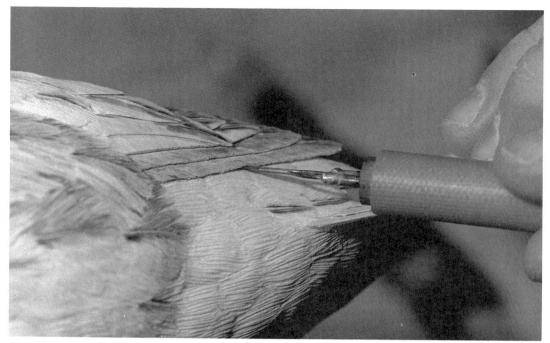

Now he uses the burning tool to undercut the primaries. This step thins the edges of the feathers and creates separation between the primaries and the feathers below.

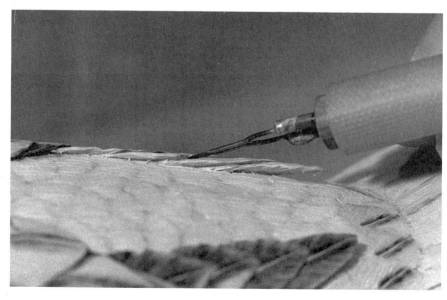

Don continues undercutting the primaries, this time on the inner portions of the feathers.

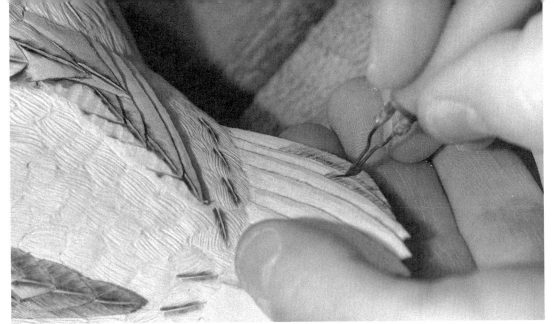

He does no stoning on the tail area, leaving the feathers smooth and rigid looking. In this photo he is placing a split in the second feather from the outside by cutting through it with the burning pen, exposing the feather below. Such imperfections add greatly to the realism of the bird.

Don has burned a split in the second and third feathers. On the third feather, the forward portion of the feather appears to be beneath the rear portion. Real birds often show such evidence of wear and tear.

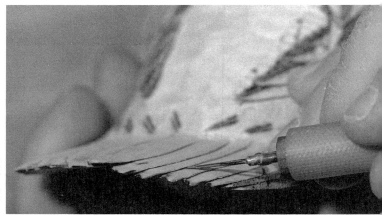

Now he uses the burning tip to undercut the edges of the tail feathers, providing separation and definition.

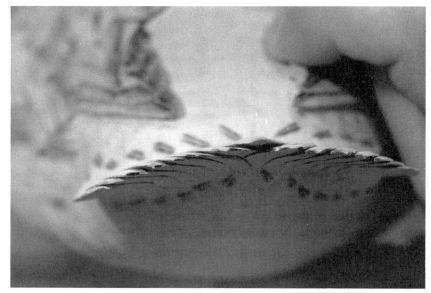

This rear view shows the separation of the tail feathers.

An upper view of the tail feathers, with burning complete.

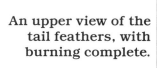

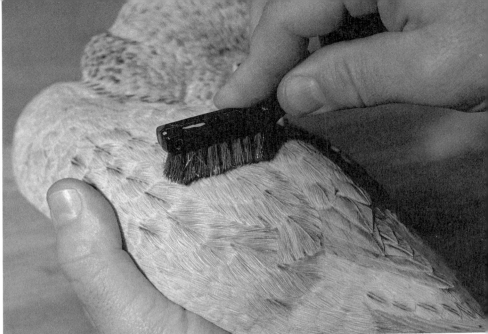

Before sealing and painting, Don cleans the burned areas with a stainless steel brush. The brush removes charred wood and dust and prepares the surface of the wood for sealer and paint.

Detail of the completed primary feathers, showing quills and barbs.

The neck of the bufflehead drake is fluffed out because the bird's head is in a low, sleeping position. Don used the burning tool to give the feathers on the back of the neck a slightly puffy look by etching deep detail lines.

Detail of the wing area with the bill tucked under. Note the texturing technique along the edges of the wing.

The opposite side of the wing, showing flow patterns of feathers along the wing and upper breast.

The completed bufflehead drake showing the bird's right side . . .

. . . and the left side.

The painted bufflehead pair.

2
Dan Brown
Feather Detail for a California Quail

When Dan Brown began carving birds thirty years ago, there were no how-to-carve books, no videotapes, no seminars with leading artists. So Dan learned to carve by "just doing it."

He was born in Dover, Delaware, grew up on the Nanticoke River in Maryland, and spent as much time waterfowl hunting as he could. An interest in carving and collecting decoys came as an extension of hunting. "There were a lot of canvasbacks on the river in those days," he says. "I'd go out and find some old wooden canvasback decoys floating on the river and I'd bring them home. They weren't worth much then, but I liked them. I'd been collecting decoys for years before I realized I was a decoy collector."

In those days, you could buy a Ward Brothers decoy for $10 to $15, and you could buy Ira Hudsons for $5 or $6. Dan bought decoys to hunt with and to admire after the season had ended.

He began carving to make decoys for his own rig, and to repair some of his favorite hunting decoys. He visited Crisfield often and soon came under the spell of Steve and Lem Ward, who carved masterful decoys in their little workshop.

"I played semi-pro baseball in Crisfield, and later I was there a lot as a salesman for Pet Milk. It got so every time I went to Crisfield I'd go see the Wards, and then it got so I'd not only go see them, but I'd spend the day there."

By the late 1960s Dan was finding a market for his birds, and in 1968 he left his job with Pet Milk and devoted full time to his carving, which by then had evolved from making working decoys to creating more intricate, decorative carvings. "Lem always encouraged me to develop my own style and my own patterns," says Dan, "but my birds looked like his for a long time. I was so totally exposed to the Wards that when I made a bird I made it like theirs because I thought that was how a bird was supposed to look. But gradually I began to develop my own style. There were no books on carving then, and if you wanted to carve you had to pick up a lot of it on your own. It took me years to get rid of a lot of bad habits."

Although there were frustrations in having to learn on his own, the lack of technical instruction forced Dan to develop his own techniques, such as his method for making feet from wood and solder as ex-

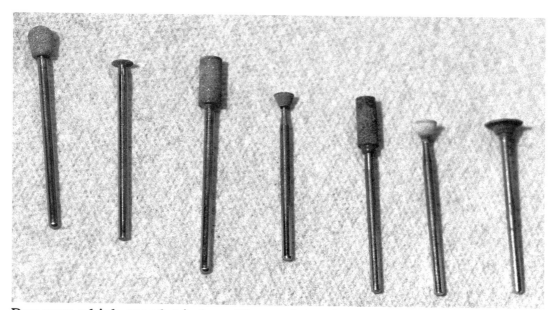

Dan uses a high-speed grinder with a variety of bits to texture the quail. Bits of various sizes and shapes are needed to texture different areas of the bird, and the different shapes produce a wide variety of textures. Shown in this photo are, from left, a round diamond stone, a small sawblade-type cutter, a cylindrical diamond cutter, an inverted cone, a cylinder-shaped red stone, an inverted white stone cone, and a red stone disk.

plained in an earlier book in this series. Dan also has been active in teaching others. He has written chapters in several books, has taught seminars and conducted countless public programs, and writes a regular column on carving techniques for *Wildfowl Art Journal,* which is published by the Ward Foundation.

In this demonstration, Dan textures a California quail using a variety of stones mounted in a high-speed grinder, then he adds fine detail with a burning tool. Basically, the procedure calls for using the stones to carve feathers and feather groups—to create the little lumps and bumps that provide the illusion of softness—and then to add feather barbs and quills where appropriate with the burning tool.

Dan advises carvers to pay scrupulous attention to reference material, to study live birds, photographs, and taxidermy specimens before carving, texturing, and painting. Texturing, says Dan, is not simply a random series of carved feathers and burned quills and barbs. Texture must follow the flow and pattern of the real bird.

"It helps to have mounted birds and close-up photos of live birds," Dan says. "These show the shape and flow of the feathers, and with them you can produce a lifelike carving."

Before he textures the body of the quail, Dan makes the plume from a piece of solid-wire solder. The first step is to use a hammer to flatten the metal.

Then he uses a metal grinder to taper the edges of the solder and shape the plume.

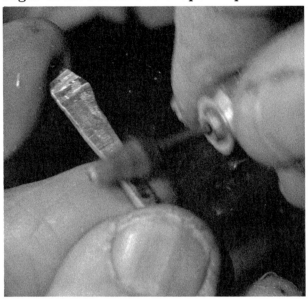

Dan uses the hammer to coax the solder into the approximate shape of the plume.

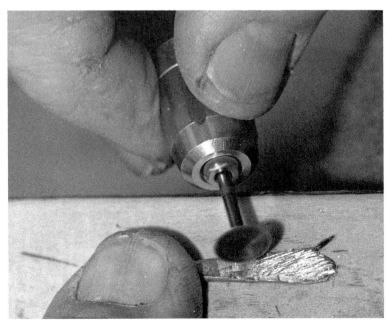

Now Dan uses a saw-type cutter to texture the solder. Referring often to a photograph, Dan replicates the pattern of feather texture in the quail's plume. He warns that care should be taken when using this sharp-edged tip. For safety, the rotation of the blade should push the tool away from the fingers holding the workpiece.

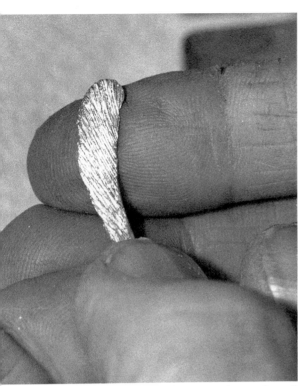

The plume is now shaped and textured and is ready to be attached to the quail's head.

Dan drills a small hole and glues the solder into place. Now he is ready to texture the rest of the bird and prepare it for painting.

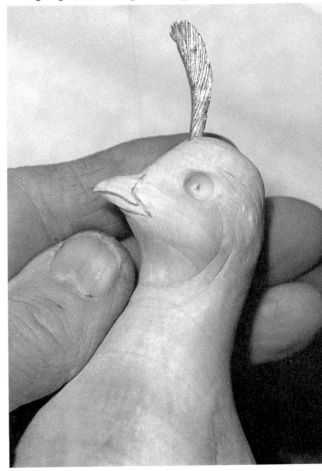

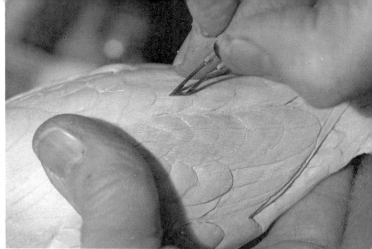

Dan uses a burning tool to add feathers to the back of the California quail. "The feathers are very fine there, so I burn the primaries, tertials, and most of the back," he says.

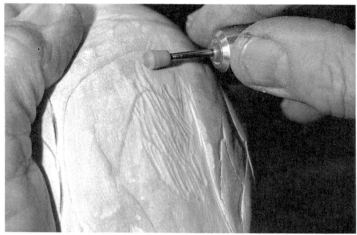

He uses the round diamond stone to texture the breast of the quail. "With this round stone I can be very bold, very free, and make nice puffy areas."

The diamond cylinder is used to create fine feathering over the more coarse texture produced by the round stone. Dan uses the sharp edge of the cylinder to cut feather detail.

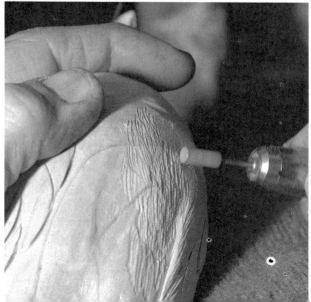

The diamond cylinder is also used to texture the flank feathers. "The flank feathers are usually heavier and more loosely laid," says Dan. "I get a really rough cut with the cylinder, and then go back over the area with the burning tool."

Here he uses the burning tool to add fine detail to the rough texture produced by the diamond cylinder.

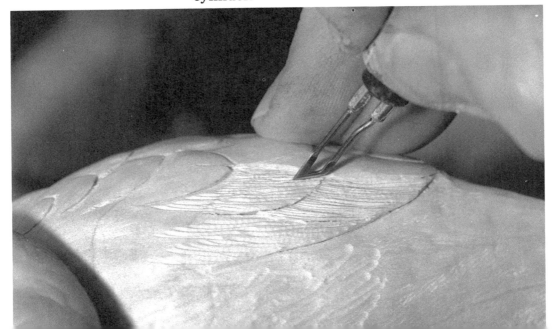

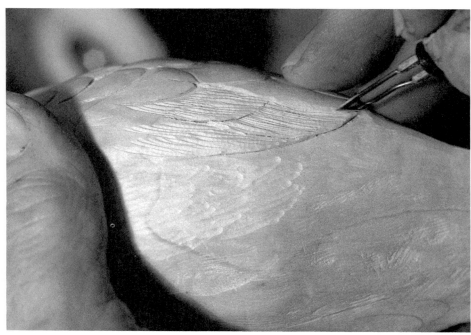

Dan's procedure is to create rough texture and some subtle lumps and bumps with the diamond cutters, then to use the burner to replicate exact feather detail over the textured foundation.

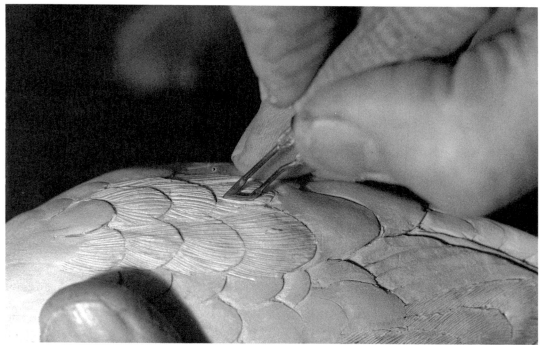

Here he textures the side feathers after they have been ground with the diamond stone.

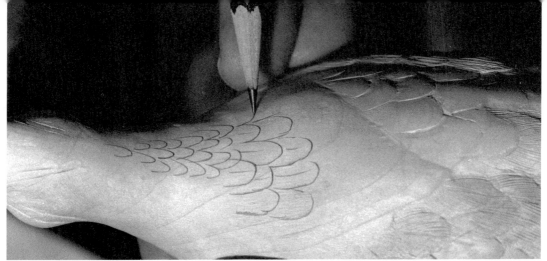

Before Dan begins texturing the neck of the quail, he uses a pencil to sketch the position of overlapping feathers. "I pencil in the feathering in areas where I'm not going to carve feathers," he explains. "This ensures that my design will be right before I begin the texturing process." Dan refers to the photographs or taxidermy specimens to determine the size of the feathers, which become increasingly larger as the back broadens. Here Dan sketches the quills, or shafts, of the larger back feathers.

Before texturing the back, he cleans his burning tip with a piece of fine emery cloth. "It's very important to keep the tip clean. The charred resins from the wood have a tendency to build up and cause an insulating effect, and the tip won't heat as well."

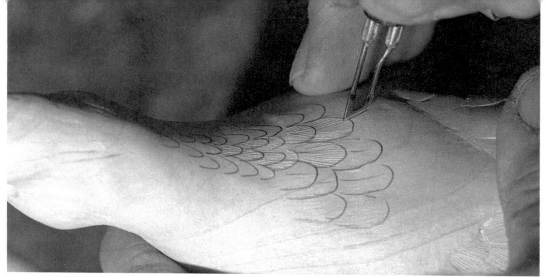

Dan begins burning the feathers on the neck and back. "You should burn this area very lightly," he says. "The lighter you burn, the better the area accepts paint. If you burn too deeply, the burning actually chars the wood, so the wood absorbs more solvent from your paint and causes an uneven finish." To provide the illusions of contour and softness, the feather lines should not be perfectly straight, but should have a slight curve, depending upon the area in which they are located.

This photo shows the completed primaries, tertials, and tail feathers.

Texture along the breast is fine, with no quills or feather shafts, only the burned feathers overlaying a stoned surface.

This close-up shows the carved and textured feathers along the flank of the quail.

The textured bird is now ready for gesso, which
seals the pores of the wood, and paint.

A close-up of the head, showing texturing around the neck and eye.

The completed California quail.

3

Grayson Chesser
Texturing a Crow with Rasp and Gouge

Grayson Chesser became involved in decoy carving through a childhood passion for waterfowl hunting, and now, at age forty-three, the two pursuits are so closely interwoven they are impossible to separate. Grayson enjoys hunting because it gives him a chance to prove the quality of his decoys in the field. And he enjoys decoy making because it is a logical extension of hunting.

At some point in the early part of this century, most decoy carvers began making birds with the buyer in mind rather than the bird. Grayson belongs to the earlier generation; although his decoys are more often purchased by collectors than hunters, he still carves for the eye of the bird, not for the eye of the buyer.

Grayson lives on a farm on the Eastern Shore of Virginia, a narrow peninsula that separates the Chesapeake Bay from the Atlantic Ocean. The area is rich in the traditions of waterfowl hunting, and Grayson keeps this legacy alive. During the waterfowl season he spends many hours hunting black ducks and brant on the seaside, teal and mallards in the bayside creek near his home, and snow geese and Canada geese in soybean fields on the upland of the peninsula.

At season's end, you can find Grayson in his carving shop, using unsophisticated tools to make incomparable decoys that are at once contemporary and traditional. In this session he carves and textures a crow using hand tools such as a rasp, chisel, spokeshave, and knife. Before the advent of high speed grinders and burning tools, decoy makers often produced the illusion of feathers by texturing the wood with hand tools such as these. Many decoy makers who enjoy the traditional aspects of waterfowl hunting prefer to stick to the old ways of texturing, as Grayson does here.

The side profile of the crow is cut out on the bandsaw. Grayson does as much of the rough work as possible on the saw; here he cuts the outline of the head and opened bill.

Grayson carves the crow from a plank of sugar pine about four inches thick. The bird will be twenty inches long and about five inches tall. Here he sketches the outline of the bird freehand. The crow will be in an open-mouth, calling position.

The top view of the crow is then sketched freehand, using the center line as a guide.

Once the outline of the bird is cut, Grayson uses a pencil to sketch a center line down the length of the bird.

With the top view sketched, Grayson returns to the bandsaw and cuts away excess material from the sides of the bird.

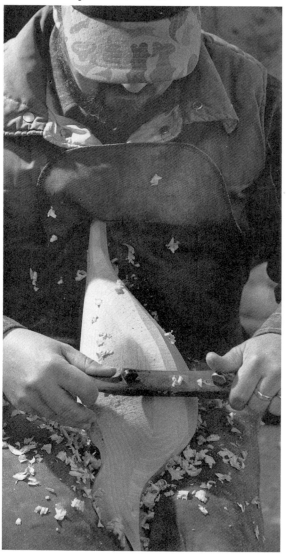

The shape is refined with a large spokeshave, which is used here to round off the body of the bird.

Now that the crow is roughed out, Grayson uses the bandsaw to round off the edges. He warns that extreme care must be used when attempting this procedure on a bandsaw. For safety, you might prefer to round off the bird with hand tools.

He uses a knife to remove material under the neck where the spokeshave will not reach.

The spokeshave rounds off the area under the tail.

Grayson uses a Stanley Surform rasp to round out the bird and to remove flat areas left by the knife and spokeshave. The rasp marks create a featherlike texture that will remain in some areas.

The Surform rasp rounds off the top of the head, removing knife marks.

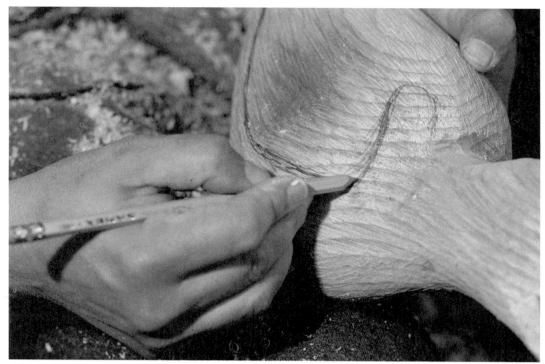

With the bird roughed out, Grayson is ready to add detail. Here he uses a pencil to sketch the wing edges on each side.

The next step is to use a sharp knife to cut a line along the pencil mark. This line will be about one-quarter of an inch deep and will form the lower edges of the wings.

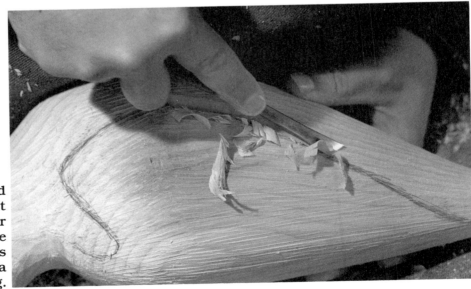

A chisel is used to back-cut along the lower body to the knife line, thus creating a raised wing.

The chisel also is used to define the V-shaped area where the wing tips fold above the tail.

Now Grayson sketches the rump area and the underside of the tail.

He cuts along the line with the knife, then backcuts along the tail to give the impression that the wings rest on it.

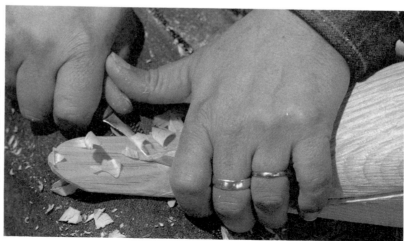

The undertail area is easily seen in this photo.

The knife is used to round off the edges of the wings.

Grayson then begins work on the head and bill, here using the knife to round off the upper mandible.

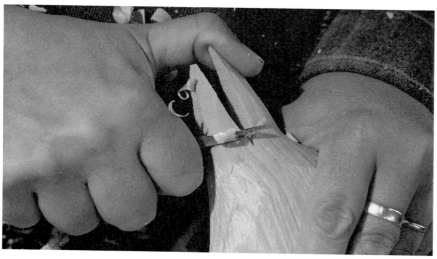

To carve the lower mandible, he removes wood and rounds it off with a sharp knife.

A knife with a long, sharp blade is used to cut an eye channel, which separates the cheek and the top of the bird's head. Grayson makes this cut on both sides of the head. He is careful to align the eye channels, viewing the bird from the front to ensure that the channels are parallel and of the same depth.

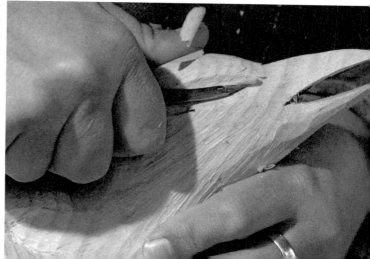

The pencil defines the area where the bill meets the head. Grayson sketches detail such as this to make sure it is correct before carving.

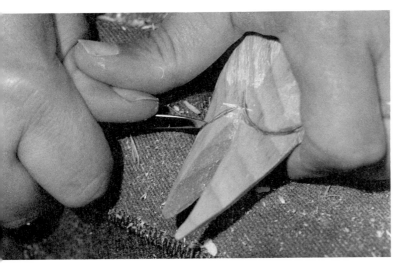

And now Grayson uses the knife to cut along the pencil line.

As he cuts back along the bill toward the line, the bill begins to take shape and definition.

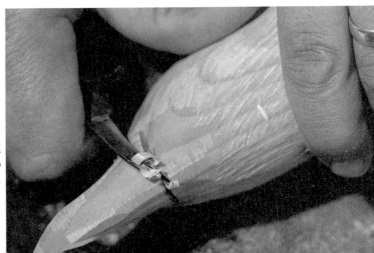

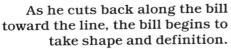

Before refining the shape of the head Grayson determines the eye placement and cuts a depression to accommodate the glass eyes. He uses a pencil to establish the position of the eye. If the placement does not look right, he will erase it and move it slightly.

Instead of using a drill, Grayson uses the knife blade to carve the socket for the glass eye.

Before inserting the eyes, Grayson finishes carving the bird. First he uses the spokeshave to remove excess wood and round off contours.

The rasp is used along the head to create feather detail. By changing the angle of the cutting edge, Grayson can vary the size and depth of the markings.

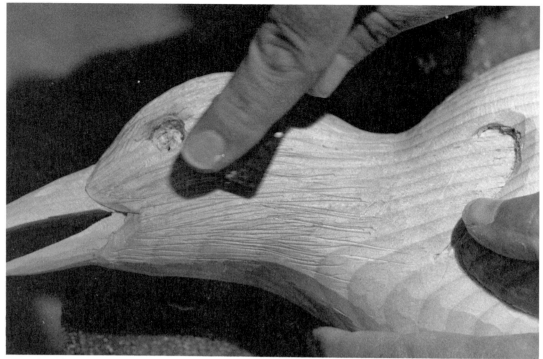

The half-round rasp follows the curves and contours of the crow, creating a pattern of feathers.

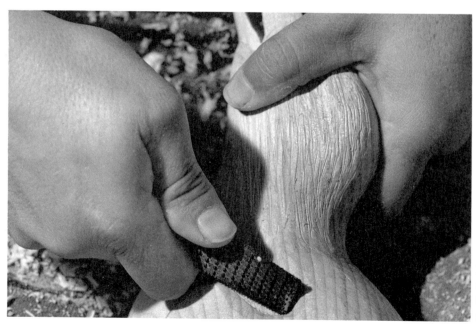

Finer lines
are used along
the head and
neck of the bird.

Bolder lines are used along the breast and wings.

Additional detail will be added by a small triangular gouge, which Grayson uses to cut shallow lines along the neck.

The combination of rasp and gouge lines looks like this. Texturing provides important detail when carving a bird like the crow, which has no bold color patterns.

After the eye is added, a half-inch dowel is inserted into the bottom of the bird, and it is mounted on a piece of rough wood. The crow is mounted in a "scolding" position, with its head slightly lowered.

The next step is to paint the bird, and although the crow is uniformly black, care must be taken in the painting process. Grayson uses Rustoleum flat black paint and dilutes it slightly with paint thinner. His goal is to create a slightly translucent black, which will easily show the feather texturing.

If the paint is too thick, it will appear opaque and hide the subtle texture marks left by the rasp, but if the paint is thinned slightly, it will give the illusion of translucency.

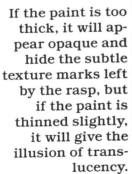

An important step in achieving this is burning off the excess black paint. Again, a thinned coat will not block up detail. Burning helps the paint quickly soak into the wood, rather than forming a layer on top of it. After burning, Grayson polishes the bird slightly with a soft rag. Be sure to do the burning away from other flammables. Keep a fire extinguisher handy.

The finished crow, textured in the traditional manner with rasps and gouges.

4

Grayson Chesser
Comb-Painting a Pintail

Prior to the days of sophisticated detailing tools, decoy makers developed some effective methods of adding feathers to a decoy during the painting process. Although feathers and feather patterns could be painted on, the effect was much more effective when the detail was actually etched into the paint, and that's what we'll be doing here.

Many old-time carvers used a technique called scratch painting; they applied a base coat to the decoy, allowed it to dry, and then painted on a top coat and used a sharp tool to etch detail into the paint while it was still wet. With this technique, the top coat is scratched away to reveal the color of the base coat.

Combing is much like scratch painting, but instead of etching one feather at a time you comb entire groups. As Grayson demonstrates in this chapter, he first applies a base coat of flat black, allows it to dry, then applies a top coat of smoky gray. While the paint is still wet, he uses a small metal comb to scratch through the wet coat of gray, revealing the black coat beneath. The effect produces a nice imitation of feathers and creates a handsome herringbone pattern.

Comb-painting has been with us for at least a century. Decoy carvers apparently borrowed the technique from 19th-century furniture makers who used graining combs to produce the illusion of grain on painted furniture.

In this session, Grayson will comb-paint a pintail drake. He begins by applying two coats of Rustoleum flat black as an undercoat. He will start combing when the second coat of black is dry to the touch but not hardened, so that the comb will slightly indent the second coat of black as well as the gray top coat. For finer vermiculation, Grayson allows both black coats to harden completely.

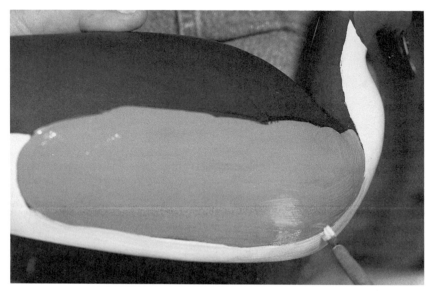

To begin the finish coat, Grayson paints the sides and breast white, then paints the sidepockets a smoky gray, which is derived by mixing raw umber tube paint with Rustoleum white.

While the paints are still wet, Grayson uses a brush to blend the edges of the gray and white. It's easier to do this one area at a time. Start on the left side, then do the top, then the right side.

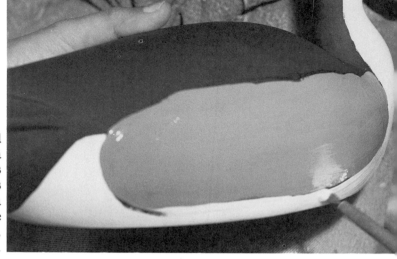

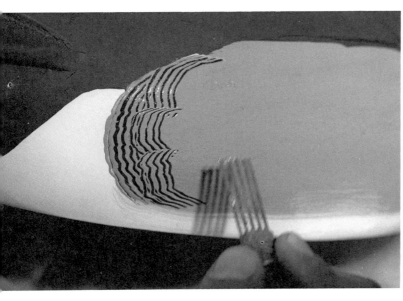

He begins combing with a small metal graining comb attached to a wooden handle. Graining combs are available through carving supply dealers, or you can make your own by using part of a plastic comb. He commences at the back of the bird so the feather patterns overlap.

By painting before the second black undercoat hardens completely, Grayson creates a bold pattern of vermiculation, which is just right for this pintail. "Ducks such as mallards and canvasbacks have finer vermiculation, so you would alter the technique slightly for them," he says. "For fine vermiculation, let the undercoat harden completely, and combing will produce a fine line."

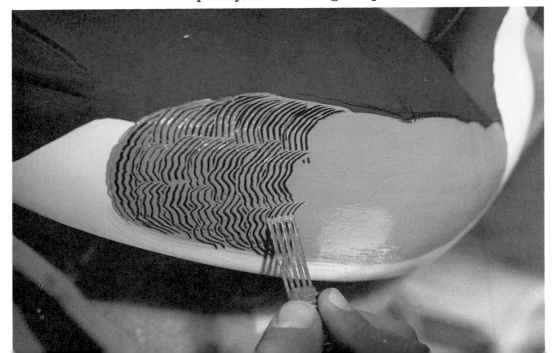

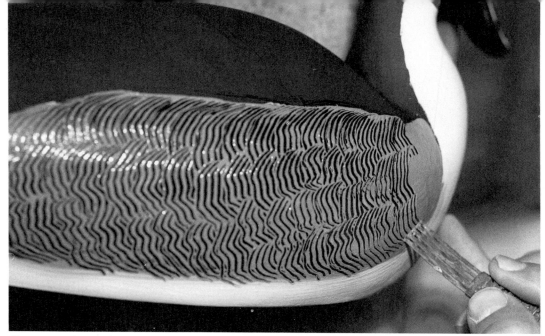

Grayson has almost completed the right side of the bird. He always does the right side first, then the back, then the left side. "I pivot the bird on my knee as I paint, and by painting in this sequence I always have the painted area moving away from me," he says.

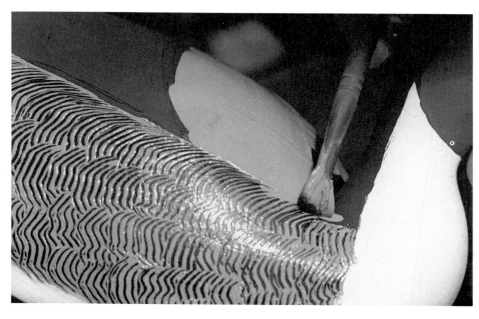

Now he paints about three inches of the pintail's back with the same grayish mixture of raw umber and white.

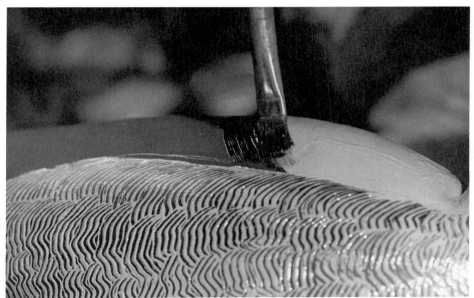

He paints the rear portion of the back with flat black, blending it into the gray.

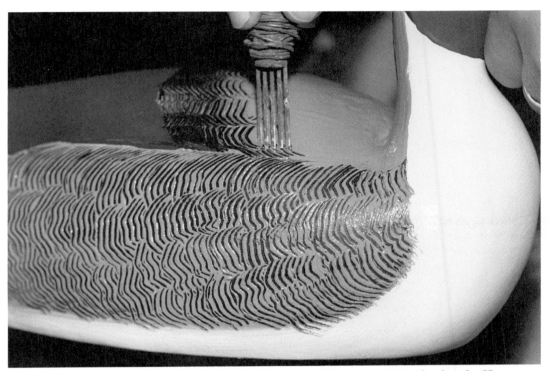

Now Grayson is ready to texture the back. He begins combing at the rear of the painted area and moves forward, overlapping his strokes.

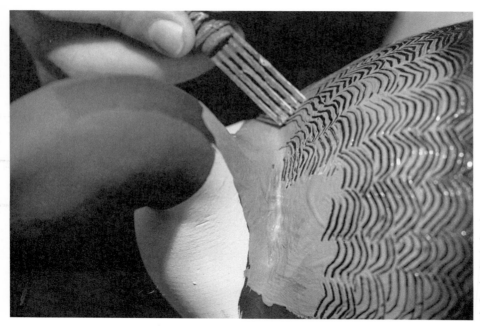

The smoky gray color extends up the back of the neck as well, and this entire area will be combed.

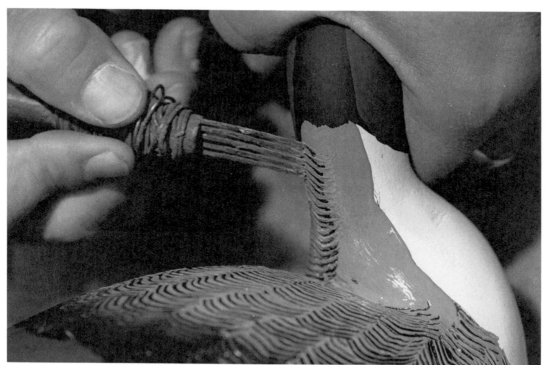

The gray area extends up the neck approximately to the same area as the white along the breast.

With the back done, Grayson begins painting the second side.

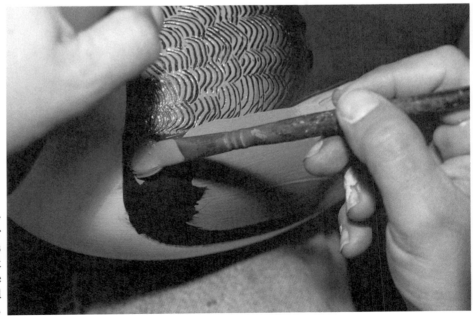

The gray side-pocket color meets the edges of the breast and back. These areas should not be blended.

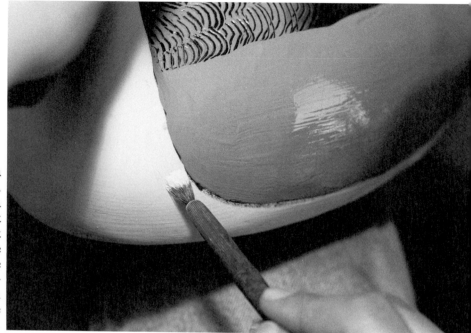

As he did on the first side, Grayson uses a small amount of white paint to blend the white of the breast and lower sides with the gray of the sidepockets.

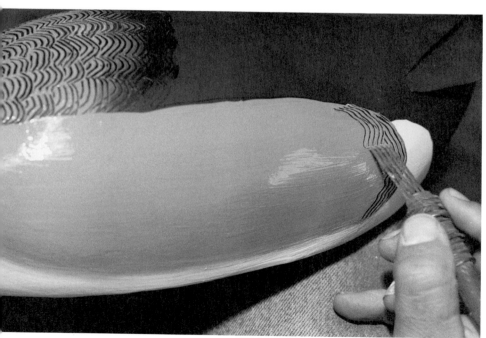

He begins texturing the second side, again starting at the rear of the sidepockets.

70

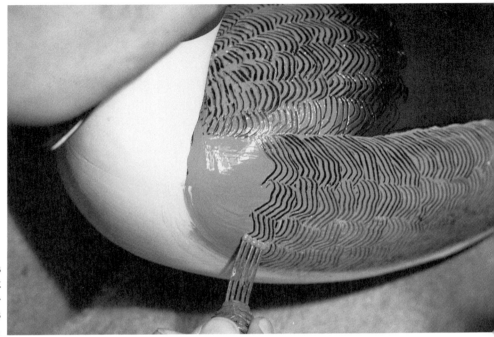

As he finishes combing the left side of the pintail, texturing is nearly complete.

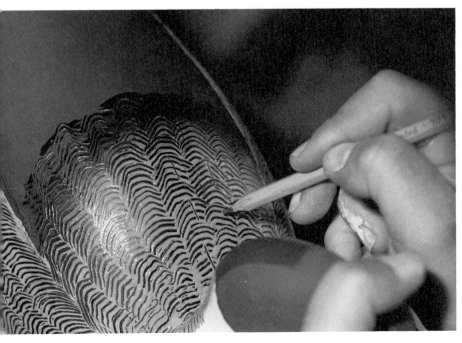

While the paint is still wet, Grayson will use a soft lead pencil to indicate feather shafts and to open up any combing lines that might have become filled with paint.

The complet-
ed pintail
sidepockets.

The finished pintail drake. Grayson's carving shop
is in the background.

5

Rich Smoker
Burning and Stoning a Decorative Scaup

Rich Smoker brings to bird carving a background in waterfowl hunting and taxidermy, two pursuits that have taught him a lot about the habits and anatomy of waterfowl.

He grew up in Selinsgrove, Pennsylvania, hunting ducks in local ponds and along the Susquehanna River. A need for hunting decoys led him and his father to carve a rig of black ducks, mallards, and canvasbacks while Rich was in high school, but he didn't begin to carve seriously until 1979, when he opened his own taxidermy business and began using his slack season to carve.

"Other than that hunting rig, I made my first decoys for a contest in 1979, and began my first decorative a year later," he says. "I realized I could carve decoys, but not the way I wanted to, so I kept working at it. I knew the anatomy of the birds through taxidermy. I knew what they looked like from the inside out, but it was hard for me to take a piece of wood and make them look right from the outside in. I had no art education or background. I learned about mixing paints and using an airbrush in taxidermy training. When I finally discovered that carving had a lot in common with taxidermy as far as the sculptural aspects are concerned, I realized that carving wasn't as hard as I thought, and I began doing more of it and started to sell some."

Rich and his family moved to Crisfield, Maryland, in 1983 and he began to spend more time carving and less time doing taxidermy. In 1985 he quit taxidermy completely, except for preparing his own study skins.

Since then, Rich has won more than 230 ribbons in such competitions as the Ward World Championship in Ocean City, Maryland, the Mid-Atlantic in Virginia Beach, Virginia, the Havre de Grace and Chestertown shows in Maryland, the spring and fall shows in Chincoteague, Virginia, and numerous others. His gunning decoys and decoratives are in collections around the country.

In this session, Rich demonstrates his stoning and burning techniques in texturing a scaup drake. Basically, it's a three-step procedure. First he uses a pencil to sketch individual feathers, feather patterns, and little imperfections such as splits and overlaps. Once he's satisfied with the feather design, Rich uses a high-speed grinder with a variety of bits to create subtle feather contours and shapes. This stoning technique provides the foundation for the third step, the carving of individual feather barbs with a fine-tipped burning pen.

Much of the realism of the bird comes from these early stoning and burning sessions. For example, Rich uses fine stones to create feather splits, and he adds

Rich's first step in texturing the scaup is to sketch feathers and patterns. Establishing the feather layout with a pencil allows him to create a pleasing composition before making it permanent. At this stage, he determines the location of feather splits and overlapping feathers.

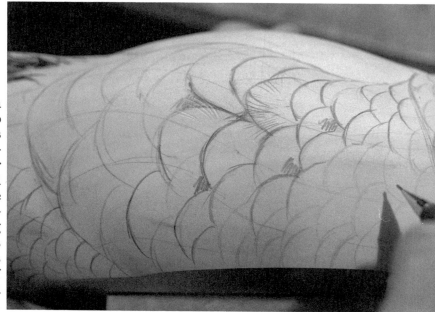

subtle wrinkles to the primary and tertial feathers. In nature, birds are not perfect, and small faults such as these make the bird appear more lifelike.

The effects are amplified during painting. Washes of paint darken the feather splits, creating the illusion of shadows, and Rich will paint shadows in the subtle valleys he creates in the primaries and tertials, thus giving depth and dimension to the bird. (Rich demonstrates his painting technique in Volume 6, *Bird Carving Basics: Painting*.)

Rich begins by sketching, stoning, and burning the sidepocket feathers. Then he carves the breast feathers and creates quills and barbs along the folded wings. He ends the demonstration by stoning and burning feather detail on the head. These techniques can be applied to any bird. Refer to live birds, study skins, and photographs to determine the size, placement, and flow of the feathers.

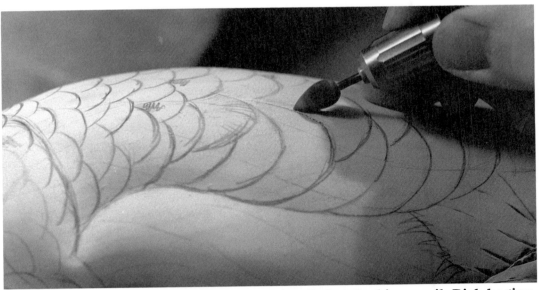

With feather detail sketched in pencil, Rich begins relieving each feather group with a pear-shaped fluted cutter. "I use this tip on a high-speed grinder to open up the deep areas between the feathers," he says. Rich cuts along each pencil line, removing just enough wood to provide relief.

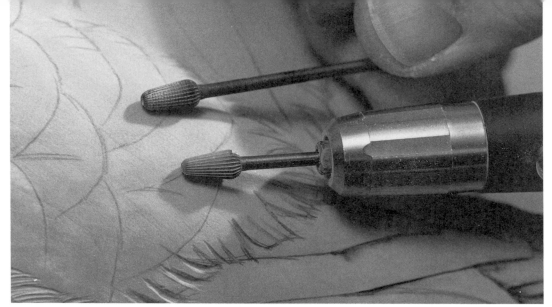

He uses a variety of cutters on the high-speed
grinder. A cross-hatched fluted cutter (top) is
designed for fine work, while the small stump
cutter (bottom) removes wood more rapidly.
"When carving small, subtle feather groups, I use
the fluted cutter. If I need to remove wood quickly,
I'll pick up the stump cutter," he says.

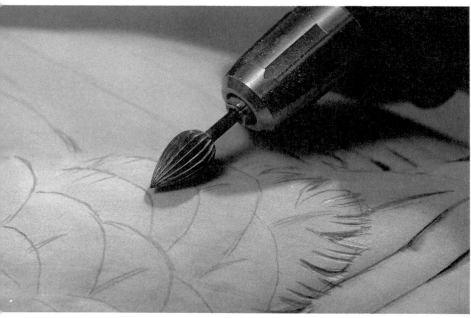

The pear-shaped
cutter is used
to relieve large
feather groupings,
such as these
on the wings of
the scaup.

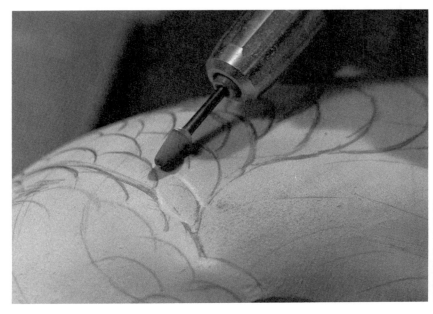

Here Rich uses the fluted cutter to create slight channels between feather groupings along the breast.

The purpose here is to create a slight contour to distinguish each feather or feather group. Says Rich: "I cut down the area behind each feather, then the front of the feather, to avoid having a fish-scale appearance. You want to create a gentle flow from one feather to the next."

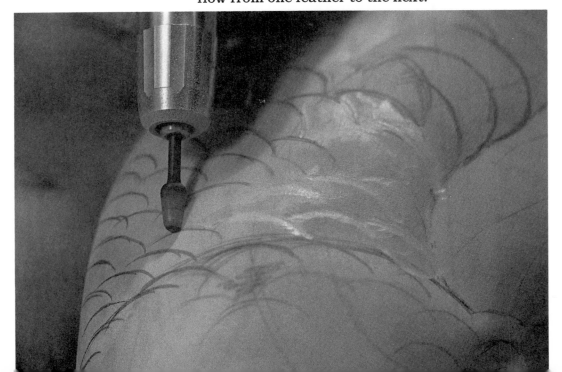

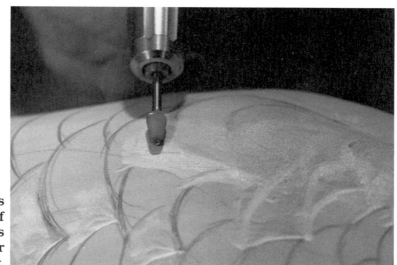

The stump cutter is used to round off and soften the edges left by the larger pear-shaped cutter.

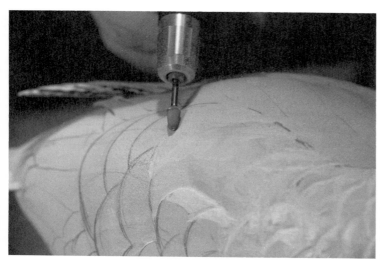

The fluted cutter is used to smooth the edges of the feathers. You want just enough depth to create subtle relief; too deep a cut will appear garish. Remember, the separation of feathers and feather groups will be enhanced later in the burning and painting steps.

Once Rich creates feather contours, he goes back with the pencil to reestablish the feather edges.

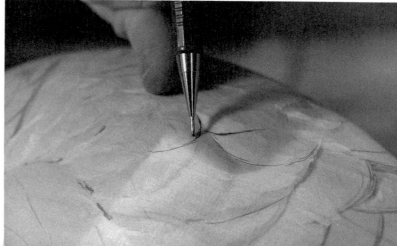

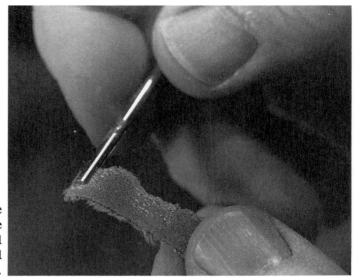

The bird must be sanded before fine detail is applied to the feathers. Rich sands with a small piece of 220-grit paper attached to a small split mandrel.

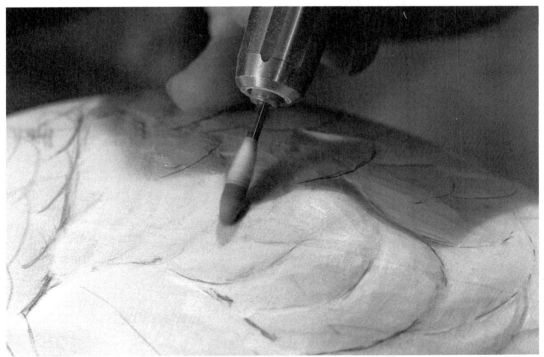

He inserts the mandrel in the high-speed grinder and begins sanding the smaller feathers.

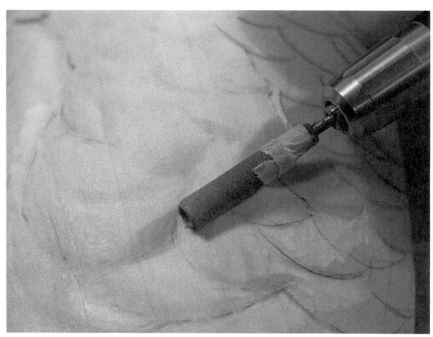

For the larger feathers and feather groups, Rich uses a larger mandrel and a larger piece of 220-grit paper. "This allows me to sand the larger areas without leaving sanding marks that might be created by the smaller mandrel," he says.

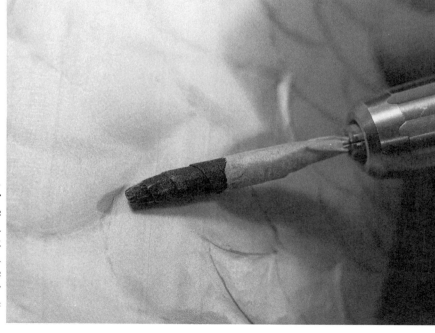

For a fine finish, Rich goes back over the area with the large mandrel and a piece of 400-grit sandpaper. The goal here is to remove any tool marks or scratches left by the coarser sandpaper.

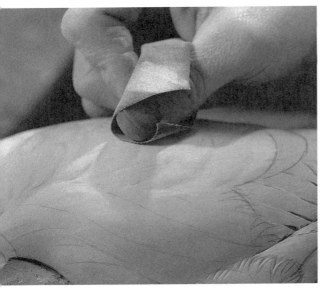

Rich finishes the sanding job by lightly going over the area with a piece of 400-grit paper. "I always go back over the feathers to knock down the top edges and make sure the feathers flow together properly."

Again, Rich uses the pencil to reestablish the edges of the feathers. Because the feather definition is so subtle, the pencil lines provide an important visual guide when Rich adds more precise feather detail in the following steps.

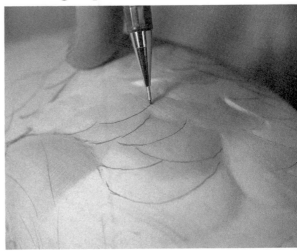

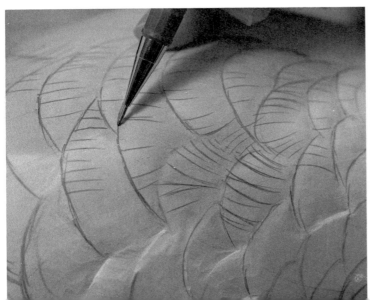

Rich sketches flow lines and feather splits with the pencil. In these areas, top feathers will be carved with slight separations, allowing the feathers beneath them to show through.

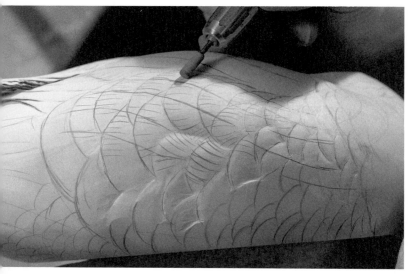

Rich uses a stone on the high-speed grinder to begin defining the feathers and feather splits. He uses a variety of stones to cut along each pencil line.

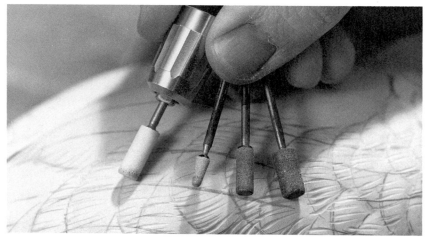

These four tips are all used during the stoning process, depending upon the location and the shape of the feathers.

Once the splits have been cut with the stones, Rich cleans the area with a "de-fuzzer," which closely resembles a small pot scrubber used in the kitchen. This tool is available from most carving supply dealers.

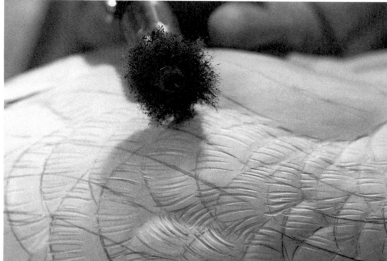

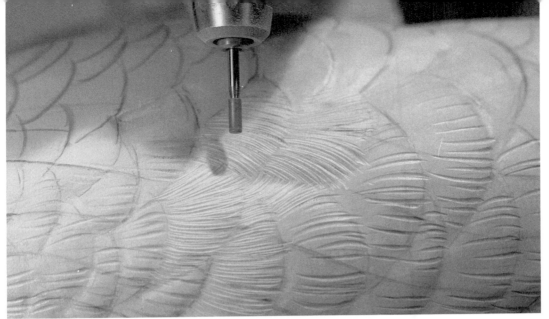

He uses a very fine diamond cylinder stone to carve feather barbs. Notice the pattern and flow of the barbs on each feather. Good reference materials such as sharp photographs, live birds, and study skins are essential in establishing the shape, size, and flow of the feathers.

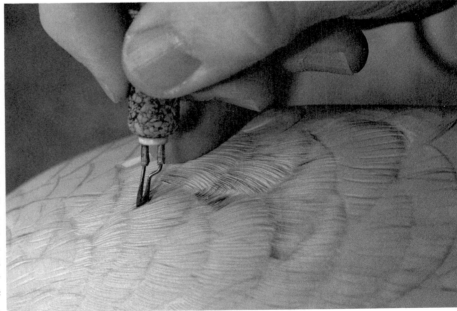

Rich uses a burning tool to carve the finest feather barbs. This tool is similar to a soldering iron, but it has a sharp, bladelike tip and a thermostat to control the temperature of the tip. The hot, sharp tip of the tool cuts a very fine line. The finest tips can produce one hundred or more lines per inch.

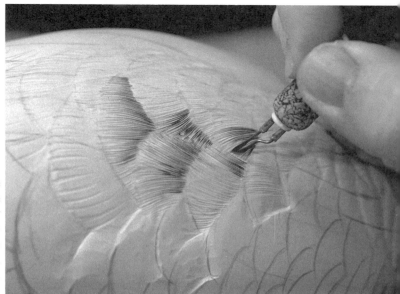

The burned lines, like the lines carved with the diamond stone, follow the feather patterns established in previous steps. Here, Rich burns a cross-hatch pattern where two feathers meet.

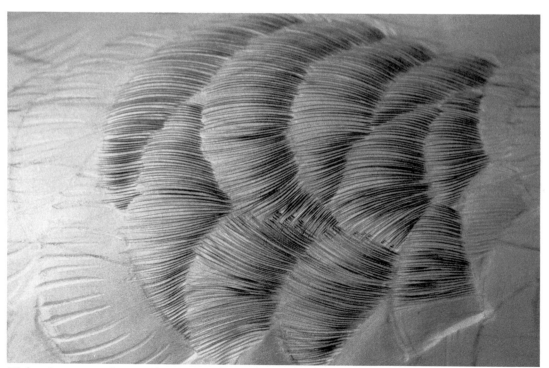

This close-up shows the area Rich has burned along the sidepockets of the scaup. Notice the area in which feathers overlap.

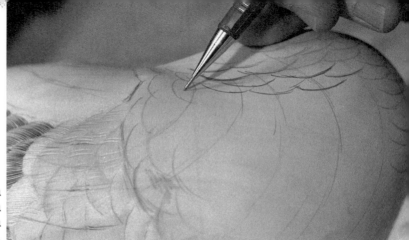

With the feathers burned on both sides of the bird, Rich sketches the feather pattern on the breast.

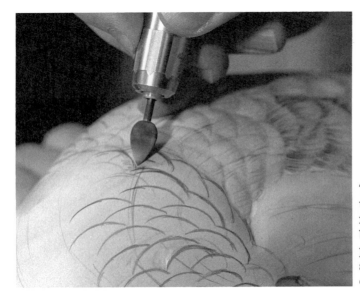

The pear-shaped cutter is used to relieve these large feathers on the breast. As before, Rich follows the pencil lines, making a very shallow cut to establish a contour for each feather.

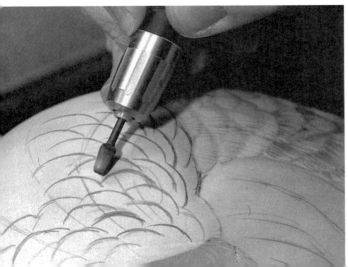

The stump cutter is used to soften the edges left by the pear-shaped tip. "The goal," he explains, "is to add some texture to the breast rather than leaving it slick."

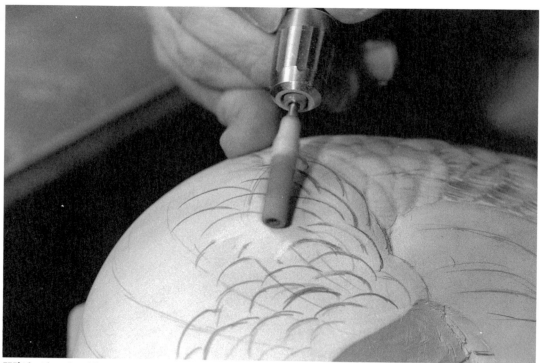

With the feathers carved, Rich smoothes the area with a piece of 220-grit sandpaper in the split mandrel.

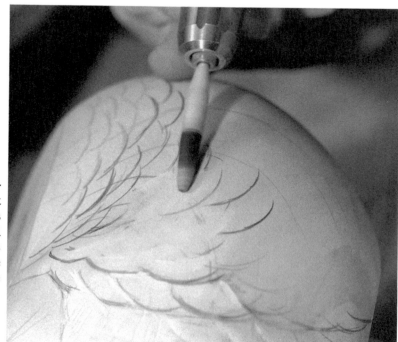

A second sanding with 400-grit paper removes tool marks and any scratches that might have been left by the 220-grit paper.

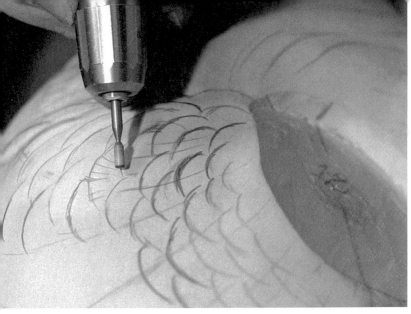

A small white cylinder stone is used to cut feather splits on the breast of the bird.

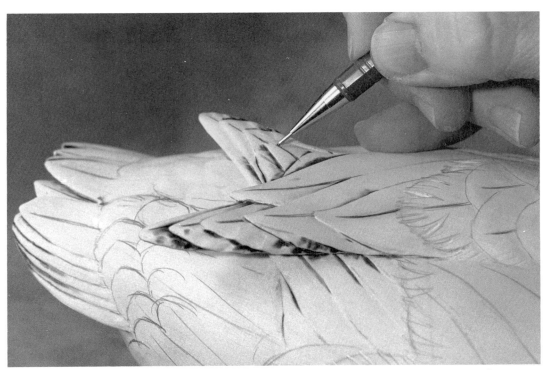

Now Rich is ready to begin texturing the primary and tertial feathers, which are folded across the back of the scaup. Here, he uses the pencil to sketch the quills that are visible on these feathers.

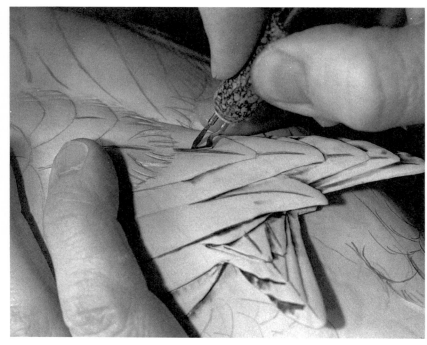

The burning pen is used to carve the quills. Rich makes two parallel cuts with the tip, one on either side of the pencil mark. The raised area between the two cuts will become the quill.

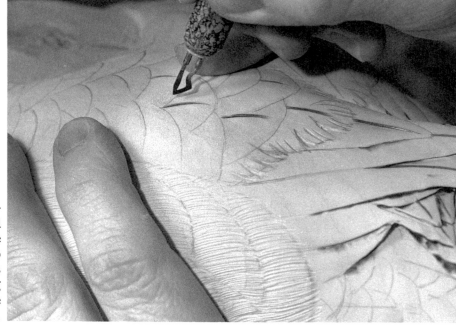

The same procedure is used here on the scapulars. Two parallel cuts with the burning pen create the quill.

The quills are further defined by burning the outside edges of the lines. "As you burn, pull the tip away from the quill," says Rich. "This softens the edge of the line and makes the quill more prominent."

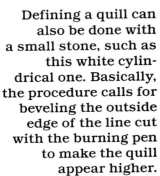

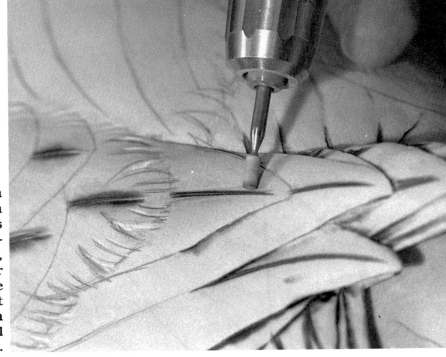

Defining a quill can also be done with a small stone, such as this white cylindrical one. Basically, the procedure calls for beveling the outside edge of the line cut with the burning pen to make the quill appear higher.

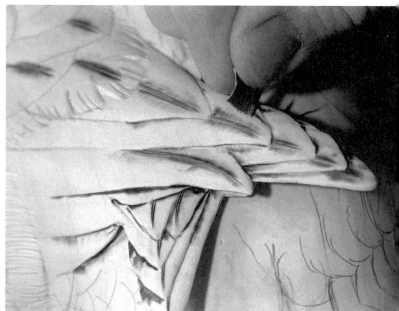

Rich uses a small piece of sandpaper to remove charred wood from the quills. In a few minutes he will burn individual barbs into the feathers, and the quill must be clean and well defined so he can see it clearly.

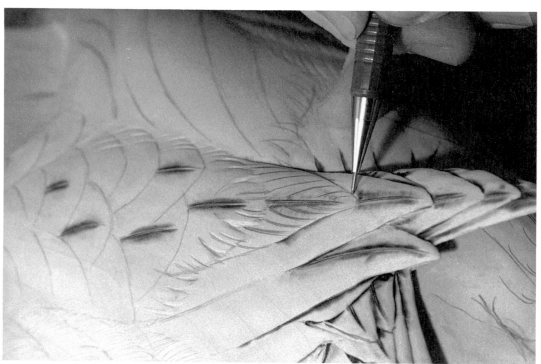

Before adding more texture Rich sketches feather flow lines on the primaries and tertial feathers.

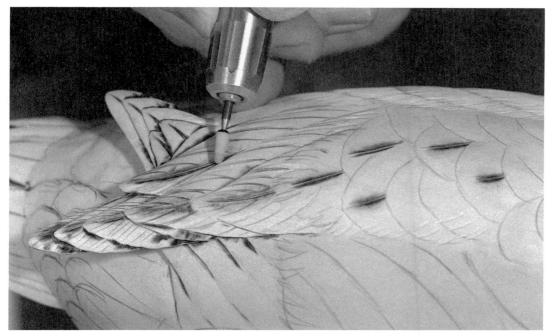

Using a stone with a rounded tip, he adds some "valleys and ridges" to the tertial feathers. "These will give the feathers some interest, some contrast, so they won't all be alike and won't all be perfectly straight and flat."

The artist at work. Rich's work area is well lighted by incandescent and natural light, and a wide variety of tips for his high-speed grinder is kept close at hand.

With the quills in place and some stoning accomplished, Rich begins burning each feather barb on the primaries and tertials. Each cut begins at the quill and extends outward to the edge of the feather. The groove is slightly deeper at the quill, where the feather is thicker.

As he burns the tertials, note that the barb lines curve slightly, in keeping with the contour of the feather. A close study of live birds or study skins will reveal that most of the feather barbs are curved.

Rich burns feather barbs over the texture added earlier with the grinder. This gives a slightly wrinkled appearance to the feathers, providing an illusion of softness and loft.

Before he adds feather barbs to the primaries, Rich uses a hard white stone to add ripples to the edges of the feathers. This detail will be amplified in the painting process. "The ripples help me create some shadows and highlights when I paint, rather than making it monochromatic," says Rich. "The valleys will be shaded slightly, giving the painting depth."

With the stoning completed, he burns feather barbs onto the primary feathers.

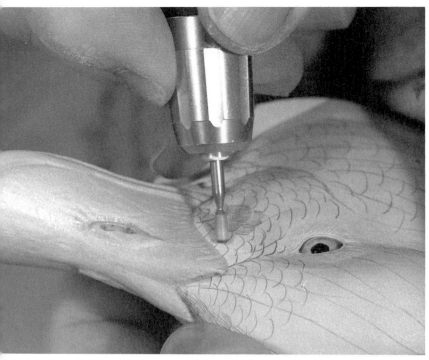

Now he is ready to texture the head of the scaup. After sketching the small feathers behind the bill and along the cheek, he uses a small white stone to add detail. "What you're doing with this stone is embossing the wood," says Rich. "The edge of the stone is rounded slightly, so it doesn't actually cut into the wood, but instead compresses the wood fibers."

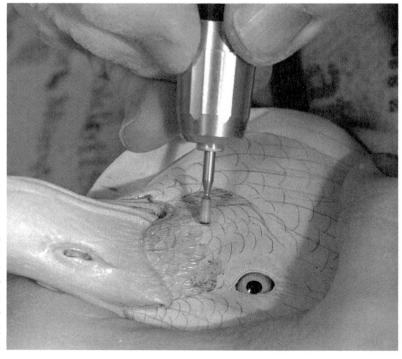

The detail is cut into each feather in a fan-shaped pattern. Check your reference material to ensure proper feather shape and flow patterns.

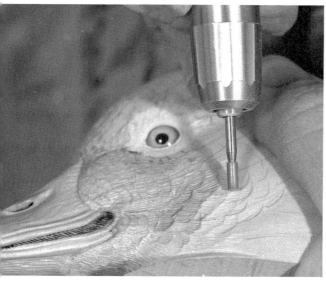

Here Rich has switched to a harder diamond stone to add feather detail. "This stone will cut the wood, even though its edge also is slightly rounded," he says. "Tupelo, which I'm using here, sometimes has a lot of grain, and the white stone will ride over it. The diamond cylinder will cut through it. You don't want the edge too sharp, though, or it will dig into the wood too deeply."

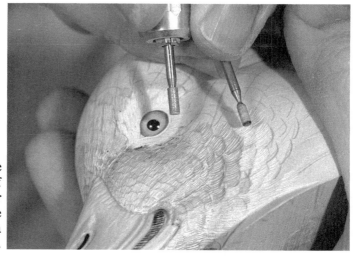

The two stones and the partially textured head of the scaup. The harder diamond stone is on the left, the white stone is on the right.

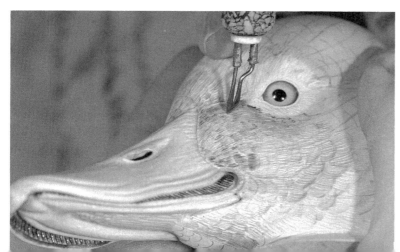

Once the feathers on the head have been stoned, Rich goes over the area with the burning pen, adding still finer detail.

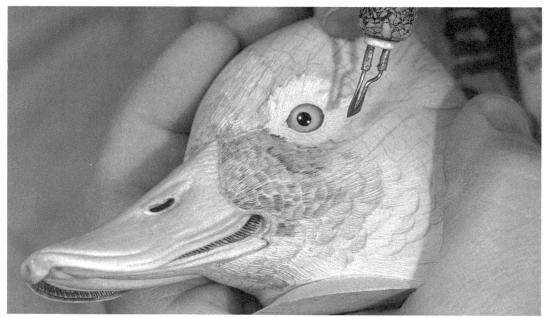

The tiny grooves made by the burning pen follow
the feather pattern established by the stones.

The scaup drake showing the effects of burning
and stoning on the breast, sidepockets, face, primaries, and tertials.

About the Author

Curtis Badger has written widely about wildfowl art, wildfowl hunting, and conservation issues in general. His articles have appeared in many national and regional magazines, and he serves as editor of *Wildfowl Art Journal,* which is published by the Ward Foundation. He is the co-author of *Painting Waterfowl with J. D. Sprankle* and is currently working on a book about salt marsh ecology.

Other Books of Interest to Bird Carvers

Songbird Carving with Ernest Muehlmatt
Muehlmatt shares his expertise on painting, washes, feather flicking, and burning, plus insights on composition, design, proportion, and balance.

Waterfowl Carving with J. D. Sprankle
A fully illustrated reference to carving and painting 25 decorative ducks.

Carving Miniature Wildfowl with Robert Guge
Scale drawings, step-by-step photographs and painting keys demonstrate the techniques that make Guge's miniatures the best in the world.

Decorative Decoy Designs
Bruce Burk's two volumes (*Dabbling and Whistling Ducks* and *Diving Ducks*) are complete guides to decoy painting by a renowned master of the art. Both feature life-size color patterns, reference photographs, alternate position patterns, and detailed paint-mixing instructions for male and female of twelve duck species.

Bird Carving Basics: Eyes
Volume one in the series presents a variety of techniques on how to insert glass eyes, carve and paint wooden eyes, burn, carve with and without fillers, and suggest detail. Featured carvers include Jim Sprankle, Leo Osborne, Pete Peterson, and Grayson Chesser.

Bird Carving Basics: Feet
Volume two features the same spectacular photography and detailed step-by-step format. Techniques for making feet out of wood, metal, and epoxy, creating texture and tone, and shaping feet in various positions are demonstrated by Dan Brown, Jo Craemer, and Larry Tawes, Jr.

Bird Carving Basics: Heads
Volume three illustrates how to create realistic head feathers by various methods, such as burning, wrinkling, stoning, and carving flow lines. Experts like Jim Sprankle, Mark McNair, and Martin Gates share their innovative techniques.

Bird Carving Basics: Bills and Beaks
Techniques such as burning and wrinkling, inserting a bill, using epoxy membranes, making open and closed bills and beaks, and carving the tongue are demonstrated.

Bird Carving Basics: Painting
Full-color close-up photos illustrate painting methods in detail. Features techniques for vermiculation, iridescence, creating an aged patina, and painting in layers.

For ordering information and a complete list of carving titles, write:
Stackpole Books
P.O. Box 1831
Harrisburg, PA 17105
or call 1-800-READ-NOW